How I Made My First Film Living On the Streets

"A DREAM IN MOTION"

By Abike O. Washington

ABIKE TALENT COMPANY

How I Made My First Film Living On The Streets « A Dream In Motion »
Copyright © 2016 by Abike O. Washington

For information contact :
Abike O. Washington
http://www.abiketalentcompany.weebly.com

Book and Cover design by Designer
Title ID: 6731298

ISBN-13: 978-1540490063

Photo Credit
Colby Phillips

First Edition: November 2016

CONTENTS

Dedicated ToMyCollegeInstructors

This book is dedicated to the few instructors that helped me realize that I had within me ideas and talents I knew not of. Thanks!!!

GENE POUNCY, ELCENTRO COMMUNITY COLLEGE – DALLAS, TX for reminding me daily that excellence's the key.

MICHELLE POULIN, UNIVERSITY OF NORTH TEXAS – DENTON, TX for helping me to realize that I had very good ideas and that I could take them and put them into an expression.

RANDY LOFTIS, UNIVERSITY OF NORTH TEXAS – DENTON, TX for telling me that you believed that I had the ability to go on to become a great writer and that if you did not believe it, you would not have told me so.

PREFACE

Why? Why did I write this book? And why are you reading it?
Simple, I want to share how I made my first film living on the streets. And you want to know how I did it. On the next several pages you will surely find that out. But the truth is, more than a how I did it book, I want (YOU) the reader to understand something even greater. It's something that we tend to forget in the hustle and bustle of this world and in the demands of others strongholds and desires concerning our own lives. Yet these desires are not our own. You have forgotten that although you were born in a collective world full of people, YOU ARE AN INDIVIDUAL. An individual who has forgotten who you are or, you have never really learned who you are, allowing the world's thoughts to dictact that for you. YOU ARE MORE THAN THAT. AND SO AM I. No one

is this world is going to care about you more than you. I mean really truly care about your total welfare. I am sure that you are AWAKE enough in this world now to understand what I really mean. We all have been massively lied to, deceived, tricked, plundered, raped and robbed and done over many times. But fret not! You are awakening for a reason. Allow life to reveal to you that there is truly a better life for you than the one you have always known or been told about. And then recognize all the people that will devise to try to take away that better life from you. The real truth is there will be many people from the top to the bottom that will seek to annilate you for their own reasons, not yours. There will be many that will pretentiously walk into your life, but their motivations are purely not right and they will try to deceive you, only to slight you of that true blessed place in life you so deserve. You see not only can you see it; they can too contrary to what people have told you about people not seeing your dreams and visions. We live in a spiritual world. In fact, beyond flesh and bones, we are spiritual beings. I learned that just because people are successful or rich, that doesn't mean they want to see you at the top or see you succeeding. And I learned that just because people are poor or unsuccessful, don't mean they empathize with your suffering and want to see you better your life. There will be some from the top and the bottom and everything in between trying to seek to prevent you. When I say top, I mean folks according to American success: cars, money, houses and all the means. Some have that, but have a really dead spiritual life. So they don't have true success. But in the midst of it all, try to do and be your best daily and go after your own dreams and goals. BE WELL, DO WELL & MOST OF ALL TRY YOUR BEST TO HANG IN THERE AND KEEP GOING INSPITE OF. NEVER GIVE UP!!!!!!

Written with love and care, Abike O. Washington

A Chapter in My Life:

TURNING THE PAGE

I'll start with the year 2010. I was attending The University of North Texas located in Denton, Texas. My major was print journalism with a minor in sociology. And it was during this time that Spike Lee was scheduled to speak on November 11, 2010 8:00 p.m. in Winspear Hall at Murchison Performing Arts Center. I had no idea he was coming. A week before the actual event a classmate of mine, Cody Pennington asked me would I like to go see Spike Lee. I said yea where. He said here on campus, I'll get us some tickets. I said cool.

Now here we are at the event. The house was packed, because it was not only opened to students, it was opened to the public. Everyone and their mama were in the house. When I say packed, I don't think there was an empty seat at all. But because of my classmate Cody, I had the best seat

L

in the house. I was dead center, front row seat in Spike's face. I somehow felt this was one of those moments, in what we like to call a divine appointment. Not to mention that I was a print journalism major and I had a profile story due for my class in a few days. Who better to profile, right! So I'm in the house, pen and pad, ready to go. On stage he enters, the crowd goes crazy. And I'm thinking that's Spike Lee. Again, I knew this was a special moment for me, so I gave my undivided attention.

Now before I continue forward, can I say something off topic a moment? My girls were in the house too. We all had a journalism class together. As we met up, I noticed that we all had on grey and black or either silver on. How is it that people, in this case (my classmates and I) came dressed in the same exact colors, black and grey? We had no idea what the other would wear or what colors. But we all came in similar fashion. I just had to point that out. Back to story...

So Spike is speaking. You can tell he has said his speech many a times to many a colleges before. But he is so in the moment that nothing was boring or stale about it, and yet profound. So profound that I took what he had to say to heart.

He first starts his speech by reminiscening on his beginning years when he attended Morehouse College, a predominant black historic college located in Atlanta, Georgia. His advisor realized that his grades where low and that he had no more electives available. They insisted that he select a degree program soon.

"I did not choose film, film chose me, I wanted to ball, said Lee, filmmaking is not work to me because I enjoy making movies."

After graduating from Morehouse, he decided to attend the Tisch School of Arts graduate film program. He made a film titled "Joe's Bed-Stuy Barbershop: We Cut Heads," which won a student academy award. Film school is where he became a filmmaker.

"No one is going to hire you because you have a degree, said Lee, they want to see the films you directed, produced or the scripts you wrote, admonished Lee."

Then a little later his speech would become more in depth. "You do not want to be in a position in five, ten, twenty years from now where every day you get up and drag yourself out of bed to a job that you don't want to be at, and where they really don't want you at. Most people go to their graves having slaved on a job their whole lives, you don't want to do that."

Then he later continued, "So the key is to find out what you love and want to do with the rest of your life."

I still have that profile speech assignment to this day. During my time at UNT and even after I left, I would pull out that profile paper that I done for my journalism class and I would read it over and over again. I took the message to heart and it was taking hold of me. I cannot put the whole speech in here. But I am putting the above key portion in here that I wrote, because this is the part that was so meaningful to me at that time. It is the part of the speech that got me to thinking about my own life and what was I really going to do with the rest of my time on earth.

Now all of it registers today. But then it was the above words that really hit home for me. When he talked about working on jobs you really don't want to be on, I knew exactly what he was saying, because I, Abike had spent almost 20 something years doing just that. And now I was at a place where I was in school, but jobs were scarce. Surviving off financial aid was the thing when I was in school and pretty much the same today.

I can't tell you how many jobs I've worked on and hated being there. I was just flat out right bored or many times the folks were always nit picketty, which then led to misery on the job. And not to mention, underpaid most of the time.

I also cannot tell you that when I WOKE UP, how many of my years had been stolen living in a mental state merry-go-round cycle of looking for a job, working, being mistreated, loosing a job, starting all over again. Looking for a job, working, being mistreated, loosing a job and so forth. Honestly many of my years, and youthful years were wasted

L

stuck in this mental place in my life.

The truth is many are manipulated and deceived and fall victim to this vicious path. I once did. All was not lost though; much of the experience I would learn from these jobs was preparing me for two necessary elements in my life: (i) To develop a mindset in me to take control of my life and to rise up and own my own business. (ii) The skillset to do it.

I use to pray and get totally frustrated, because I had three small kids that I was struggling to keep food on the table for. I was also struggling with my own life not seeming to move forward.

From the age of sixteen to being in college in my mid-thirties, I struggled with being on jobs and not really moving forward or having any real progress in life on these jobs.

While I was attending UNT and receiving financial aid and taking out loans, I was applying for job after job, but nothing was opening up. So I would take my financial aid loan money and pay my rent. During a break between school semesters, I got a little behind on rent. I assured the leasing office lady that I would have the full amount in two weeks and I could pay everything in full. I even went into my school account to show her the date that the money would post.

She ended up evicting me any way. And so I went to court and there they were, the leasing lady and the judge, evicting me. But this same woman had the nerves to try to talk me into signing another lease. See my rental contract was up the next month. She was really trying to manipulate me hard, adding that she would give me half off rent the first month. My spirit was still. And something said, do not sign another lease, it's not right.

So when my money came, I paid the apartments everything I owed them. I knew I had no where to go, but I also knew not to sign another lease. I knew that if this lady had a care in her bones she could have waited two weeks for my aid to come. I hadn't ever been late on my rent there. Also, I lived in Dallas and would commute to Denton, Texas during the week for school and I'd be there all day. These people were going into my apartment while I was gone. I could just sense and know it.

So, I just knew the situation was not right at all. I decided to move on from there and to California I headed. Skid Row "Scared Straight" was the first thing I saw straight off the greyhound bus. I like to have had a fit!!

I never in all my life living on this earth ever saw anything like skid row before. You talk about homelessness at its worst. At least in my opinion. And to be honest I still felt for me that it was a fact, not opinion. On 6th, 7th, and 8th streets it was pure human urine and feces. People were living in it and around it like it was absolutely normal. Like it was a flower garden! Even dope dealers hanging out thuggin and business men walking right through it like it was Wall Street or something.

I thought what in the world is this. It took me a minute to calm my nerves. My first instinct, mind, or whatever you call it was like run, run, run. What the hell you waiting for RUN! Well I didn't run, but I did make sure that I got the heck away from that area as soon as I possibly could. Needless to say I stayed in Los Angeles a few months, and then headed on back to Texas with a one-way greyhound bus ticket.

Still on the streets, back in my hometown Dallas. No where to go, no job, no resources, just here. I and my homeless bags. Everything around me was echoing you are going to fail. You will not make it through this. This is it, you are not young anymore. You lost your opportunity on life. You will not make it; you will not be anything but on these streets. Every negative stimuli and force you could think of was coming at me. When you are low the attacks are worse.

I was around all these angry, some drug addicts, some sexual perverts, some just disadvantaged in life like I was. But whatever the case, I knew I could not sit around all day looking at these folks and them looking at me. That was not going to get any of us anywhere.

And not to mention, when many people are down, whether homeless, on drugs, alcohol, or a convicted felon they have this tendency to want to try to destroy you if they see you trying to do something better for your life to get out of your situation. They will try to get you on drugs, they will try to set you up and get you in trouble. If the library is your only resource, they will try to pick a fight and get you kicked out so you can't use the resources to do what you are trying to do while you are going through homelessness.

And it is not just these people; it will be your competitors that try to bring you down too. Those who feel that if you rise you will be a threat to them and their business.

You have some vicious people in this world and you must remember everyone did not get the piece of pie the right way. Some folks stole their way to the top, or step on folks head to get to the top. No one ever said that success and climbing your own personal ladder to success was easy. It is not. Not at all.

So you really have to look out for yourself while you pursue your dreams. No one is going to do this for you. This is your responsibility and yours alone. Don't let men and women, whichever fit, continue to come into your life and distract you away from your personal goals and aspirations.

So after being back in Dallas and at the library for awhile and no job coming through, I got this idea to enroll into acting classes. Yep, acting classes. You see back in 2002, an inspiration came to me about acting. I moved to San Bernardino, CA then and something very horrible happened. I went under a great, great attack and I almost lost my life. I was seriously harmed. Again, I ended back up in Texas and that's when this real homeless cycle thing started.

In 2002 when I came back to Dallas, I ended up staying with a friend that I worked with at Arch Wireless.

Off topic a little, this is the only company that I can honestly say that I enjoyed working for. I was also promoted at this company into the subcontracting department working strictly with the corporate offices in New York.

What I would learn from this job later on was that I enjoyed it so much, because I was like my own little boss, running my own show. My own small business. No phones to answer from customers, just my work and my cubicle. My office! I liked the freedom. I enjoyed the personal touch that I was able to bring to my work, even though it was assigned. It just felt totally different from sitting there answering call after call, being monitored, and feeling like I had no breathing space or creativity. So when I was promoted to the subcontracting position. I loved every minute of it, which in turn caused me to perform better.

But to get back on topic and move forward, while staying with this friend I was still suffering from that spiritual attack. I had no idea what was happening to me, I had no idea why and how it happened. I just knew that my body and mind where being brutally attacked. I had no one to talk to about it because people make you think that you are crazy or they keep telling you it's the devil attacking you.

So I was left to deal with it on my own and learn what I needed to learn from the particular incident. And believe it or not, that's how Yetunde, the short film evolved. But before we get more into Yetunde, while attending KD as a performing artist student, one of my instructors ask us to do something creative outside of what we normally do, which was acting. Some chose to sing and dance, some chose to paint, some chose spoken word poetry, and I, I chose to write a screenplay. All of our assignments would be due in one week. Yes, one week.

KD has a school library. I went into the library and checked out "The Screenwriter's Bible." A book I had read before, while I was at UNT. And in 3 days, I wrote a short titled Three Chicks & a Guy. A few years later I named it Corporate Affair.

Let me add this before I move on. KD College of Film & Dramatic Arts knows how to select some of the best known talent available. I assure you, those students that come through those doors are born-ready triple threats: acting, singing, dancing. Some go on to production and filmmaking themselves. KD also has a great curriculum and I commend that school on those qualities. But I went through hell there from jealous attacks. No matter where you go, when you are spiritually attached to people that do not mean you any

L

good. No matter what you do to try and better your life or where you go those jealous spirits will work to try to bring you down.

So our assignment is due. I went to three of my classmates and asked them to be readers/performers on stage for my script. Next thing you know, Mr. Clarke Lindsley comes racing around the corner to behold of this little short I wrote. He asked me to follow him into the classroom. There he sat, read, and then the critique followed. I knew then, I had some skills. At the time Mr. Clarke was not my instructor, I was just in my first semester and I would not take him until next term.

He informed me that I did really well and that I had a few technical errors but as far as story, I had done well. It was at this is the time; I was beginning to learn what I could really do. During community college and classes at UNT, my sociology instructors would always inform me that I had really good ideas, when I would turn in my written assignments.

Thing is I was a poor writer. GRAMMER. Probably still am. SMILE. But what I was beginning to learn is that I had the ability to put down my expression and how I viewed a topic or subject down on paper and that people were responding, even if it was controversial.

In my second semester at KD I was cast in the play Legally Blonde, the musical at the Garland Civic Theatre. But before this I was approached by two officers, one black male, and one Hispanic male and told that I better not get on the train, that I could not be successful. They said it was not for me. I was downtown Dallas, and two officers were standing in the public declaring this. I was totally shocked. I was shocked because I can understand doing things to make you unsuccessful, but actually telling you no flat out in public was astonishing.

I boarded the train anyway. When I arrived at the audition, I checked in and met with the theater artistic director, Kyle McClaran. Then after check-in I went outside and prayed. I made my plea known. I was tired of the attacks that I had been through for so many years. Attacks so vicious, that they were really a hindrance to the earlier half part of my years. I just wanted to do something. Something better in life.

After the audition was over, I left, thinking that I would not be cast, because I was told that I would not get it, by those cops. A few days later, I was sent an email. I had been cast for two roles. Excited I was indeed!!

I went to every rehearsal and was always on time. Two days before it was time to perform, I was arrested and taken to jail at about 3-4am in the morning for trespassing. You see, I was living on the streets and I would sleep inside the DART rail station to keep warm from the cold. I would get up early and head to school, then afterwards to rehearsals.

I never got to be apart of the play. I was a no show. I called my cousin from jail and asked to please call the theatre, ask for the director and explain to him what happened, to please tell him that I was sorry. When I got out of jail, I went to the theater to explain. He wasn't there. I don't know if he ever got the phone call or the letter that I left with the front desk assistant.

After about a week or so of being released from jail, I had enough of Texas. I had enough of the attacks. I got my little homeless bags, pawned my laptop, took the money and moved to Atlanta, Georgia. While there, I was still on the streets. I tried a shelter at first, but they kicked me out in the cold, because I stood up to them for abusing an older lady by giving her a urine-stained sheet to sleep on. I also stood up to them for threatening to throw a young lady out in the cold with her baby, because they said she had an attitude. The young lady was hysterical, because somebody stole all her stuff. All the stuff her and her child had.

I was on my mat on the floor when the cops showed up at the shelter in the late of the night. I could hear them talking to one of the staff members telling them that they don't want her here at the shelter, referring to me. I never said a word, I just laid there. Two days later, I was kicked out in the cold. In the freezing cold, in downtown Atlanta. I vowed to never go to anymore shelters. The streets it was.

I stayed focused in the midst of it all. I would sleep in Buckhead on a law firm's front porch most of the time. It would be cold and raining, but somehow, I survived. One night I had no money and it was Friday night and one of the attorneys showed up at the office. I was on the front porch.

People all around were partying, but I was hidden on the front porch to myself. He reached inside his pocket and handed me $20.00 and said I really wish you well in life. I said thanks, ran over to Publix and got me some food. While at Publix, I took the same money he gave me and bought him a thank you gift card. I wrote on the gift card that one day I was going to make it in life. That I just wanted to tell him thank you for stopping and helping me out. Because many folks are mean and nasty, and could care less.

So, I was very thankful for this man, especially since you hear the contrary about lawyers being the devil all the time. I sealed up the card and slid it under the office door. It was a mid-size firm. So hopefully he got it.

I kept auditioning and practicing the things that I had learned at KD while in ATL. I went on many auditions, got cast. But because people didn't really have the funding to make the projects happen or whatever reasons, it just never panned out. But then a college film student by the name of Romaine Phillips was casting for Bad Hair Say, a short film. I seriously thought the other girl had it, because it was laugh and play among them. But when I auditioned, nothing. Then I was told, you're Shonda, you have the lead role. Romaine said from the moment he saw me and I auditioned he knew I was right for the part.

This film would be my breakthrough film. Not just as a budding actress, but to learn a very, very valuable lesson in filmmaking. This production was my teacher. The lesson? I learned that you can take a little of nothing, not much money and you can make a really good quality short film, if you have a really good quality story.

See Romaine was a student along with his friends. This young man was so resourceful, that he knew how to take little and make a film. To break this down...

His story's theme was based off television journalist who felt she was fired from a major network due to wearing her natural hair. He took it's theme and decided to do a dramedy short film. I was the black business executive with the natural hair, working around all male executives. We looked the part, we dressed the part, most of all we brought the drama and the comedy. The internet ate it up.

But this would be only one of the many lessons that I would learn from student filmmakers and short film productions. See, I always thought that film was massive in scope, unattainable to people like me, whatever that meant. And in some part, this would have been true not just that long ago. But since the advent of digital technology that notion has been basically demolished, but only on a few conditions. You must have a great story to tell. That has not and will not change.

You can have in your possession all the technology you may. But STORY is always first. You must also have a really good crew and cast to help tell that story. It's still a collaborative art form. And you must be resourceful enough that when no one supports you in your endeavors, you support yourself. You don't need fancy expensive equipment, lots of money, connections, or a whole lot of resources. But you must be resourceful. In my case I had none of the above staying on the streets. But I was prayful and resourceful.

I knew that if I had a good story, actors and crew would want to jump on board. Because both like attaching themselves to projects that get them a little more recognition. I knew that I had to offer something in return, because I had no money to pay these folks, let alone a pot to pee-pee in literally. When I would meet these folks to talk to them, I would have my homeless bags on my shoulders. But I would never focus on that. I would focus on the story that I wanted to tell.

I was at a laundry mat in North Dallas when I came across a young man by the name of Marty Miskel who attends The Art Institute of Dallas. It was him and a few others filming young models in a laundry mat. My first mistake as a beginner filmmaker, or may I add not so much a mistake as it was timing. When I arrived back in Dallas February 2016 I attended Rack Focus 3 competition pitch session. At the time I knew I was not intuitively ready. But I learned about the competition by being there. Still no where to lay my head, I continued to work on a few stories I had in mind making, Corporate Affair and Yetunde. By the time Rack Focus 4 rolled around I was ready.

I dropped Corporate Affair and went with Yetunde. For some reason I had to get this story out. I had to make it happen! So I made it my focus and started the pre-production process. I would check out books at the library on "how to" topics concerning filmmaking. I would sit in a staircase tunnel and study my but off, taking notes. Then at appointed times, I would apply the information out of those books.

I remember when I held my first casting call at The Art

Institute of Dallas. Marty D. Miskel a filmmaking student at the time booked a room for us to use for the audition. I was totally excited. Only two people showed up. It never got me down. I treated the moment as if fifty people showed up, as a professional casting call. Those positive self-help books must have been kicking in! I was not allowing that to discourage me.

Still in the midst of it all there will be people who act like they are so interested in your project only to get into your business to see what you are doing, and then will later try to slight you or try to steal from you. These are deceivers trying to dishearten you. Some will even try to steal ideas and twist them up. Some will lead you on like they are on board to just stay abreast in your business affairs. And you can let none of it stop or discourage you. You've got to continue on inspite of.

The road to success is not a clean one. You may have character. It doens't mean everyone else does, which can sometimes make it a lonely path. But if you choose a better life for yourself. Then know the road will not and is not an easy path. Later I would hold my second casting call, but this time through social media. And again later I would hold a table read for Yetunde. People attended. A full house indeed. Again, another lesson I would learn about people tagging you along, but then flooking on your project at the last minute to knock you out the competition.

My plan was to enter this project into Rack Focus 4. Again, many of the crew that came along and acted as if they were so interested bailed out on the project at the last minute to try and knock me out the competition. They had other projects that they were working on. So, they only came aboard to pretend to befriend, then dropping the film project at the last minute. Again, they were trying to knock my film out.

You see, they knew I stayed on the streets and had no money or resources. But I did have a very good story. They lead me to think that they would be apart of the project as an editor, cinematographer, etc. They waited until the last minute of the competition deadline, and then dropped out. A few actors did the same, mostly extras in which their roles were essential to the story. I remember I was sitting listening to Tina Knowles, Bey's mother on YouTube. She was at a conference talking about her life and career and how she ended up where she is today. The one thing that stuck with me was that she had to make a choice in her life on what she wanted. She asked herself what she wanted, set a goal and went for it. Also, earlier that week I came across a quote twice from Abraham Lincoln, "Those who predict the future are those who create it." I felt very strong that the Universe and my Creator was trying to tell me something. I took heed! So I took out a sheet of paper, a pen, and I wrote down what I really wanted. One of those things was to film Yetunde and enter it into Rack Focus 4.

I knew what that quote meant. It doesn't mean it how many take it out of context. The man was simply saying to create your future you must take charge of your life. Simply put. After I wrote down what I wanted. Seeing that I had no

L

crew, I went to work. I look up people on Facebook, Production Hub, I contacted any and everybody, experienced and inexperienced. A couple days past and nothing. Then one of the principal actresses for my film, Latoya Yarbrough contacted me and said, I know a young lady, Ariawna Talton that can film for you, here's her number, give her a call. Then I got an email back from one of the people I submitted to. Another young lady, Elizabeth Harding, an aspiring filmmaker, contacted me back from a submission I sent out on Production Hub.

And from there we went. I got everyone's schedule and we shot the film in four days. The ladies worked day jobs, so I had to work around their schedules. But we got it done. Now mind you, these ladies never really filmed too much before. They were willing to jump on the opportunity and they did well for beginners. Even I was new. Producing, directing and writing my first film for production.

I had already invested $100 into Rack Focus 4 to pitch the film idea. But in order to actually be apart of the festival film competition you must have a completed filmed project and you must submit it by the deadline. I was thinking. I do not want to loose this $100. I don't want to let these actors down, because then you create a track record of starting projects and not finishing them. How did I get that $100 by the way? Honest truth. I stood at corner stores and did what pan handler hustlers do. I asked for the money.

There were only a very few people, that I could tell why I was asking for the money. Only a few that I could say, because I am making a film and I want to enter it into a competition. I found out real quick, that if you told people that, they would become jealous and tell you hell no.

There were also many people who tried their best to use their pocket change to try to manipulate me. But I did not allow that to bother me. I had learned from those on the streets who would ask money for food how these people would treat them. Many purposely would want you to beg from them just to make you feel low. They would act like they were being friendly to these people then try to let them down with a blow. They would also be very nasty and mean and tell people go get a job. They would try to manipulate me to get into my business and see what I was doing, then only to run and go tell on me to get me into trouble. I had many of them lie on me. I would sit, write and tweek my script and they would go tell the store people or the train station folks wherever I was at that moment, that I was bothering them.

They would even lie to try and get me in trouble saying that I came in their store and stole a bottle of VO5 and used the whole thing to wash my hair. I asked the store manager why she sit and lie like that. And if I really did that, as much as they work to try to drag me down, why she just didn't call the police. I am pretty happy they would have been delighted to see me with a whole bottle of "STOLEN" VO5 standing with my hair wet to put my happy ass in jail.

Trust me when you are trying to better your life and you are not a settle for the status quo person, many will do all they can to drag your life down. All they can!!!!

You see many of those people get a real joy out of

seeing you homeless and down to the ground. They love to see you beg money from them. And they love to make fun and talk about you too. So I would just say I need to get some food. Which was very true, but then I would half all the money I got and put it aside for Rack Focus. I was your unconventional producer raising money for my film and its endeavors. Then I started an Indiegogo campaign. Only three people contributed, but I used what was left after Indiegogo took their part to purchase props and whatever else that the $60.00 or so could buy. And I used my food stamps to feed my crew and actors. Yes I did. I bought pizza, fruit, and drinks, whatever they wanted. You see, I didn't sit back and wait. I was so determined not to fail. I used all the little resources I had to make my short film. I had no camera, but I got with those who did. I used everything free and whatever the small amount of money that I did come across, I would use to print scripts for actors, and bus fair for me to travel. Whatever. But I refused to steal, lie and cheat. I did it right. Just with the very limited resources I had.

L

We worked with what we had. And it worked!!!

A few years before while I was in Atlanta, Georgia I wrote a song titled, "Who Are You." Not knowing that years later, that very song would fit so well with my short film's theme. I had a young lady to sing it. And the editor that came on board layered it down on the film, along with the voice over spiritual/mental attacks with the actors. Ah, relax. Relief. I made it. I did it!!! And since film is a very collaborative art. WE DID IT!!!

And the real truth is, had I not believed, stuck in there, Yetunde would have never gotten made. $100 lost and actors would have wasted their time preparing for those roles. So, I have to really always thank my Creator for the life lesson I learned from the Yetunde Project.

But that's not all, Yetunde got nominated best actress. Yes, I played the lead role in my own film. The first film I ever wrote, produced, directed and starred in got nominated for best actress. Boy the power of never giving up!!!

Yetunde is A DREAM IN MOTION. Yetunde was the

project that let me know that not only could I do it and become great at it. It also informed me that I have the ability to do it. But before one pursues a path, a dream they have to know deep down inside. Can "I" do it? Then they must be committed at all cost in spite of any and all obstacles to go after their GOALS.

I was laughed at. Call a bomb. Called stupid. People tried to curse me with their mouths and say you are going to be like that forever on the streets. I got called bitches and hoes. Black people, my own race attacked the hell out of me. I had people using their spiritual mind and energy molesting my vagina and attacking my body trying to drag me down when I was trying to work towards my goals. The police would tell me to ignore these people. But how do you ignore a rapist.

I went through hell. But I was determined. Whatever, "I'm still gonna go after my dreams. Screw what you are talking about and trying to do.

That's the attitude that got labeled, BAD ATTITUDE. But

L

it's that same attitude that forged me to complete my film and want to work towards bettering my life in spite of what many attackers had to say.

Yetunde was not my ultimate dream. Yetunde set my OVERALL DREAM in motion. It's just like having a baby. You carry this unseen beautiful creation inside you. You don't know what it looks like. You anticipate its arrival. You dream of all the things you will do with your child. Who you will let hold it, who you won't. And then the actual day arrives, sometimes unexpected and you go into labor. The stress, the pain, the uncertainty, the hours of nerve-wrecking chaos trying to get this precious thing out for you and the world to behold.

And Ah!! She or He is so pretty! Even if the gremlin is ugly. You think it's the cutest child on earth, because it's yours and no one can convince you any differently. You totally are in love with your baby.

Yetunde was my beautiful baby. My first born. No she wasn't as beautiful as some of the other filmmakers in the competition. But she wasn't the ugliest. In fact she was so cute, that the judges gave her really good reviews and advised that a feature be made out of it. I was totally proud of my film. But no one saw the gritty part. The attackers, the jealous people trying to hold you down on all levels from poor to rich. The awful things one truly go through to make a dream happen, is never really told fully. People sugarcoat what they really go through mainly due to this society labeling one as a VICTIM when you open up and talk about the mental, physical and spiritual attacks that one truly goes through. You are told do not talk about that or you will seem weak, like a victim. Or worse, you are mentally ill, you are crazy. You are none of that my friend. You have two major problems. One, you got haters. Two, you have to learn how to overcome all that mess.

Now to change the subject at hand, of course I wanted to win best film. But I knew deep down inside that there were filmmakers in the competition who had better skills, resources, and had long time experience in this game. And

L

honestly I was so proud of the winner. I actually voted for the winner who won best film. I truly enjoyed their work. I had a really good story. But because we were all beginners our filming and editing was not up to par. I had learned the power of a $100 investment. I learned the power of believing and sticking by your story and never giving up. I learned that I could do it. I am thankful to Rack Focus 4. I am more thankful to The Creator for the life lessons. Yetunde will always be my first born child. She gave me a focus and a hope. She inspired me to DREAM BIGGER!

So how did I make my first film living on the streets with no money, no resources, no camera, and no connections? If you were reading, its all above. No gimmicks no lies. But before I even thought about making Yetunde I filed my DBA, Abike Talent Company. I was in preparation for the very moment. I had no idea that I would produce and direct a film. I was just writing scripts and wanted a business name for my creations. I knew I wanted to be taken seriously, and to do that I wanted to have something of my own, my own small business.

Going through those very hard jealous attacks from people, never swayed me. I had been reading books like "Think Big & Kick Ass" by Donald Trump. Also, later while preparing to make the film, I would study everyday Napoleon Hill's "Think & Grow Rich." I was so inspired by both books. Yes those nagging feelings and thoughts were there from those people's bad energy. They would attack the mind, the physical body and they would even try to put sickness or confusion on you. And most of all fear to try and paralyze you and yes try all the time to provoke you to anger to distract you and get you down. Their Jealousies are a pure crime!

And here's the catcher, they would justify their evil beaviors by lying saying that your thoughts are causing that. Because they think in their minds that no one knows about their mental and spiritual attacks, no one can see them practice this stuff. These awful people fail to realize that many books and including the bible have addressed these very issues. If these folks are not trying to play tricks on you to fool you into to thinking that their behavior is your fault, they trying to delude you into thinking that you are reaping what you sowed. WOW.

You can't reap an ORANGE if you've sowed an APPLE. Better hear what I say CLEARLY. Psychologies don't work on a mind that thinks!

This current election has allowed me to see just how mean and vicious people really are. How they will lie and slander you at the drop of a dime. I have watched both Hillary Clinton and Donald Trump. I have never met neither one of these people, so I don't have anything bad to say about them at all.

But I have watched how people on Social Media, The Media, and every Internet platform throw lies, accusations, slanders you name it against the both of these people. I have watched them take videos and patch them together and twist and contort these people's images.

And I have seen people lie on my life and slander me in

the same exact ways. Therefore, I chose the high road concerning this election not to get involved with all that hoophopla.

I can not hold a gossip column on two people I have never met. All I can do is listen to both and remember that both are human beings with desires. I chose to vote for myself. To vote for my own life, by getting up and going after my dreams, because at the end of the day I don't care who you put into office, they can't make billions of people on the earth act right. Just like all the laws in place in America don't stop people from breaking those laws. PERIOD.

And to make matters worse, people used the word GOD over and over to justify their gossip, slander and vicious hatreds to two very different people they have never met or held a conversation with. WOW!!!!

But I had gathered a new knowledge and a new confidence, even though I still struggle at times. Those books and their messages were and are totally inspiring.

So, you see, it's SIMPLE. No matter what situation you

L

are in. The TOTAL KEY: is DESIRE. It's what you really, really want to do in this life. Some call it purpose, some say passion, others say God's way, etc. The list goes on and on. But the truth is, no matter how many people tell you God want you to do this or that, if you don't Desire that. If you are not feeling that, you will not be passionate and you will not stick with it and give it your best. So it has to start with your own desires. Then you have to make the choice to do good in life with your desires. Now its time to study about the thing you desire to do in this life.

You may say, but I have many desires. Of course you do everyone does. But to be successful, study anyone. You first have to start with ONE THING. Then make that a success. Then begin to venture out from there. You cannot focus on all those ideas at once and bring them to light. Even women who have twins need help with those two babies. If she don't have help. One baby lacks at a time, until she can fully attend to the other, even though the mother loves them equally.

No matter your situation, start where you are at. Use the resources you have now, until you can obtain the ones you want and desire.

The only resources I had were a pen, a pad, ideas, my prayers, and a library where I could check out How To books on filmmaking. None of this stuff cost me money. If you think I am lying, listen to Serena William at YouTube.com when she states that her and her family did not have much money. But she had "A racket, a ball and a hope."

Most of all I could sense my Creator and the Goodness in the Universe rooting me on. I could sense it all saying, you can do this Abike. Even through all the physical, mental and spiritual attacks. I could sense, that it was saying I want to show you that you may don't have much, but you can start where you are and use the resources you have and forge ahead. Just get started and go from there.

You see get started no matter where you are in life and somehow the good in the universe will orchestrate people, places and things to come your way and get things done.

Yes there will still be trouble and hang ups. (Meaning some will come your way not orchatrated for you.) . But you will make it through that.

I hope this little small book have in some way inspired and motivated you to get started right where you are. To set a goal, learn about what you desire to do and just get started. Take small steps. I challenge you, stop in your life, and get FOCUSED! Get all those folks out that truly don't belong there. The one's that truly do not care about your welfare. Those that just want to hang on to your spiritual life and suck you dry. Who just want to use and take advantage of you, your reservoir and hinder you from great and wonderful things in your life for your mind and spirit.

Set a GOAL, an AIM, A DREAM. And just go for it. Your path will not be mine. Your resources may or may not be mine. Your dream may or may not be mine. But whatever it is, GET STARTED. And once you get started, STAY FOCUSED!!!

After reading this book, if it has in any shape, form or

fashion inspired and or motivated you, will you please visit my website at abiketalentcompany.weebly.com or simply Google at Abike Talent Company and make a contribution of your choice to any of my future film projects underway.

Any amount is more than welcomed and a portion of the monies you purchased this book with will go to film endeavors also. Again thank you kindly.

To leave you with my favorite quote: "A journey of a thousand miles begins with one single step." Chinese Proverb

Another Chapter in My Life:

STAY TUNED